TEN

COMMANDMENTS

Journal

Search me, O God

OlivePress
צהר זית

TEN COMMANDMENTS JOURNAL Search me, O God, *for adults*

ISBN: 978-1-941173-22-0

Copyright © 2017 by: Cheryl Zehr

Published by
Olive Press

צהר זית

Messianic and Christian Publisher
www.olivepresspublisher.com

Our prayer at Olive Press is that we may help make the Word of Adonai fully known, that it spread rapidly and be glorified everywhere. We hope our books help open people's eyes so they will turn from darkness to Light and from the power of the adversary to God and to trust in ישוע Yeshua (Jesus). (From II Thess. 3:1; Col. 1:25; Acts 26:18,15 NRSV and CJB, the Complete Jewish Bible,by David H. Stern. Copyright © 1998.)

In honor to God all pronouns referring to the Trinity are capitalized; satan's names are not.

LORD written in all capitals in Scripture signifies it is in place of:
the Sacred, Hebrew Name of God, YHVH יהוה

If you love Me, you will keep My commandments.

John 14:15 HCSB®

Table of Contents

How to use this Journal

Be completely honest with yourself in answering all the questions.

Answer as many or as few questions each day as you'd like.

Search deep into yourself in answering the questions. The purpose is to empty yourself of things that are hindering your walk with the LORD and blocking His blessings from flowing into your life.

We strongly suggest dating all your answers, because you may want to come back later, maybe even years later, and add to your answers. It will be nice to see how you have grown and developed over time.

Save room for those later possible additions to your answers.

If you are a prolific writer, you may want to write the questions and your answers in a spiral notebook, leaving whole pages blank in between for your future additions revealing how you have matured in the LORD.

Let every man prove his own work.

Gal. 6:4a

Examine yourselves, whether ye be in the faith;
prove your own selves.

2 Cor. 13:5a

But let a man examine himself.

1 Cor. 11:28a

Search me, O God, and know my heart:
try me, and know my thoughts: And see if
there be any wicked way in me, and lead me
in the way everlasting.

Psalm 139:23-24

THE FIRST AND GREATEST

COMMANDMENT:

LOVE THE LORD THY GOD

And thou shalt love the LORD thy God

with all thy heart,

and with all thy soul, and

with all thy mind, and

with all thy strength:

this *is* the first commandment.

Mark 12:30

Be totally honest with yourself:

MIND: What are my thoughts usually about?

STRENGTH: What do I spend most of my energy doing?

SOUL: What do I desire and long for most of the time?

HEART: In the depths of my being, who do I really love? Me? or God? or _____?

Thou shalt have no other gods before Me

What does this commandment mean to me?

Is the God I worship the True God of the Bible? Or is He an image I've made up in my mind?

What do I believe about God? Make a list. Then find verses in the Bible to support it. Also look for verses that might show it's not true. Check your list with Appendix I (page 84), if you'd like.

Write a prayer asking God to reveal who He truly is to you.

Now let's check our heart further to see if we are keeping this commandment.

What or who do I spend more time thinking about than God?

When I have a decision to make, who do I ask first? Is it God? List examples.

When was the last time I spent my free time with God? How did it go?

When I am afraid, what do I do first? Do I turn to God? List examples.

Is there anything I would not give up if the LORD asked it of me? Make a list and check your heart.

Thou shalt not make unto thee any graven image or any likeness *of any thing* that *is* in heaven above, or that *is* in the earth beneath, or that *is* in the water under the earth

What does this commandment mean?

How have I been keeping this commandment?

How might I have been breaking this commandment?

Thou shalt not bow down to them nor serve them

Is there anything I've made that I admire more than God and His work? List the possible things.

Am I too busy with my own work to give God any time to receive my worship? List all the things that take up your day. What can be eliminated?

Is there anything anyone else has made that I admire more than God and His work?

Do I ponder and/or admire my own words (for example, in my online posts!) more than God's Word?

Do I ponder and/or admire anyone else's words (including in posts or videos, etc.) more than God's Word?

How much time do I spend on the internet or TV or games or movies or reading novels, etc.? (These are other people's work and words.) Keep track for a week:

How much time do I spend with God and in His Word? Keep track for a week:

For I the LORD thy God am a jealous God, visiting the iniquity of the fathers upon the children to the third and fourth generation of them that hate Me

What does this part of the commandment mean to me?

When have I behaved as if I lacked love for the LORD?

"Iniquity" means the inclination to do wrong. What wrong inclinations of mine am I passing on to my children?

What inclinations did I maybe inherit from my ancestors?

How, according to this commandment, can I break this negative inheritance?

Showing mercy to thousands of them that love Me

Do I love the LORD with all my heart, soul, strength, and mind?

In Deuteronomy 7:9 it says: **Know therefore that the LORD thy God, He is God, the faithful God, which keepeth covenant and mercy with them that love Him and keep His commandments <u>to a thousand generations</u>.**

Have we reached the thousandth generation yet from the day God gave this Word?

So, is there mercy in the Ten Commandments? Where?

How has the LORD shown His mercy to me? (Make a list.)

How has the LORD shown mercy to me today? (Make a list and keep adding to it.)

Thou shalt not take the Name of the LORD thy God in vain

What does this commandment mean to me?

When do I speak the Name of my LORD and Savior with honor and awe?

When have I used the LORD's Name in a casual way?

Having a good name means the same as having a good reputation—being thought well of in the community. A father's good name is reflected in his children. A city or country's good name depends on the character of its citizens.

How have I, as a citizen of the LORD's Kingdom and a child of the King, helped the LORD's good Name?

How has my behavior hurt the LORD's good Name?

What is my attitude toward the LORD's Kingdom? How about other of its citizens?

Am I happy to let people know I am a citizen of the Kingdom and a child of the King?

How often do people hear me mention my Father and King and Savior?

Do I love the Kingdom so much that I want to show everyone how to enter it? How have I done that lately?

For the LORD will not hold him guiltless that taketh His Name in vain

Have I been feeling like I'm being punished lately? Could it have anything to do with how I've been misrepresenting God's good Name?

Remember the Sabbath Day to keep it holy

What does this commandment mean to me?

Have I been setting apart a whole day as holy to the LORD?

How can we keep a day holy?

Six days shalt thou labor and do all thy work

Do I work diligently all six other days?

Would the LORD consider me a good six-day worker? Why?

How am I teaching my children to be good workers?

What can I do to get all my work done in six days and stop working for one whole day? (For a mother: how can I lighten my work for one whole day?)

Do my children work hard enough that they welcome a day of rest from work?

What can I do to make this day special and holy to my children and not boring?

But the seventh day is the sabbath of the LORD thy God: in it thou shalt not do any work, thou, nor thy son, nor thy daughter, thy manservant, nor thy maidservant, nor thy cattle, nor thy stranger that is within thy gates:

How can I help all those around me, within my influence or under my authority to rest and be refreshed on this day?

What kinds of things do we normally do on the Sabbath that cause other people to work, serving us?

In wanting to go out, what kinds of relaxing things can we plan to do on the Sabbath that would cause the least amount of work for other people?

We don't have servants today; we have machines. They maybe don't need a rest, but does our household need a rest from hearing them run and knowing they are running?

(Exodus 35:3 says: **Ye shall kindle no fire throughout your habitations upon the Sabbath day.** Since motors are making sparks in their pistons, some people believe to obey this commandment we shouldn't use any machines on the Sabbath.} {One Hebrew Messianic-Orthodox rabbi says this is referring to the fire of strife between people.)

Exodus 16:23-29 **And he said unto them, This is that which the LORD hath said, To morrow is the rest of the holy sabbath unto the LORD: bake that which ye will bake to day, and seethe that ye will seethe.**
This sounds like part of resting on the Sabbath is preparing our food the day before even. It seems that God wanted to make sure that women also get to rest on the Sabbath.

Could this work for our family? Write a couple menus and shopping lists that would make this possible.

Imagine what it would be like if your whole community let everyone rest on the same day! Jerusalem is like that. On the Sabbath all is quiet. There are no vehicles on the streets (except an occasional Arab taxi because their Sabbath is on Friday), no machines running, no lawn mowers, no crowd noises. All stores and restaurants are closed. Very few people are on the sidewalks. No one is working. All are resting, except for those needed to save lives and keep people safe. All is peaceful and quiet. It is wonderful. It takes away all guilt to just be resting all day. It is quite refreshing and rejuvenating.

How would it feel to live in such a community?

What would Mondays feel like after resting on such a day on the weekend?

Does the LORD want me to try to create this kind of Sabbath peacefulness in my home? If so, how can I begin to do it? (The questions on the next few pages might help with this answer.) What kind of planning and preparation ahead of time would we have to do to make it happen? Use these two pages to journal your answers, being sure to date each entry. Add more ideas as they come to you. Come back in a few months and write down your progress and how these things have affected your life.

For in six days the LORD made heaven and earth, the sea and all that in them is

According to this part of the commandment, how important is it to believe that God created heaven and earth in six real days?

How can I help my children believe this in spite of the influences around them?

How does my belief in a Biblical creation enhance my Sabbath day celebration?

Does this imply that enjoying God's creation would be a good, restful activity for the day of rest?

List some enjoyable, relaxing ways to enjoy God's handiwork on this day.

And rested on the seventh day

What does it mean to me that the LORD set aside a day for *Him* to rest?

What does it mean to me that the LORD set aside a day for *me* to rest?

What all does rest mean to me?

How can I rest from inner turmoil?

How can I get my mind and thoughts to rest?

How can I rest from worrying?

What other things does my heart and mind and soul need rest from?

How can I rest from the chaos of outside activities?

What would it be like to rest from the internet and phone and all electronics for a day?

How can I accomplish that for myself?

How can I get my children to agree to this?

List here (or add to the list on page 24) other ideas of what would make this day relaxing and restful for you and your family. Keep adding to the list.

What would it be like if my whole internet community rested stayed off social media on this day? How can I possibly make this day more restful for my virtual community?

How and for whom is the LORD directing me to help make this day more restful?

Bonus question: What day did the LORD have in mind when He said the "seventh" day?

Bonus question: What other Sabbath days are commanded in the Scripture?

Wherefore the LORD blessed the sabbath day, and hallowed it

What does it mean to me that the Sabbath day is blessed by the LORD?

What kind of blessings have I received in keeping the Sabbath?

The Hebrew word used for "hallowed" means God made it holy, consecrated it, sanctified it, set it apart, devoted it, and dedicated it. What does that mean to me?

How can I make this day feel holy and sanctified and consecrated and reverent?

Deut. 5:14 ... that thy manservant and thy maidservant may rest as well as thou. And remember that thou wast a servant in the land of Egypt, and that the LORD thy God brought thee out thence through a mighty hand and by a stretched out arm: therefore the LORD thy God commanded thee to keep the sabbath day.

This chapter in Deuteronomy is where the Ten Commandments are being re-told to the new generation of Israelites just before Moses dies and Joshua is going to lead them across the Jordan into the Promised Land.

So, besides celebrating His Creation, what else does God want us to think about and commemorate on the Sabbath?

Would the LORD also like us to remember our own personal deliverances from bondage? How can I do that?

What types of bondages have I been delivered from?

What entrapments, if any, am I still bound to? Bad habits? Internet? A job you dislike? Money? Debt? Regret? Remorse? Anger? Revenge? List all the things you feel enslaved to. Ask the Lord to reveal what might be binding and hindering you from walking in true, *spiritual* freedom. Then write a prayer for God to deliver you. Date the prayers and then write the date when God sets you free and how He did it.

Jeremiah 17:21-22 Thus saith the LORD; Take heed to yourselves, and bear no burden on the sabbath day. ... ; Neither carry forth a burden out of your houses on the sabbath day, neither do ye any work, but hallow ye the sabbath day, as I commanded your fathers.

What would it do to people's backs, if all their lives there was one day a week in which they carried no heavy load?

What physical and *spiritual* burdens am I carrying? List them on another piece of paper. After pondering and praying, write them in the correct columns here.

<u>From the LORD</u>   <u>Not from the LORD</u>
(my job, raising my children, etc.)   (See also the second question below)

How can I lighten the burdens from the LORD on the Sabbath?

Jesus said Matthew 11:28-30: **Come unto me, all ye that labour and are heavy laden, and I will give you rest. Take my yoke upon you, and learn of me; for I am meek and lowly in heart: and ye shall find rest unto your souls. For my yoke is easy, and my burden is light.**

What burdens am I carrying that the LORD would like to reveal to me are unnecessary? Could it be extra stress that comes from: perfectionism; from always wanting to be in control; from worry and fear; from unreachable goals for me, for my spouse, for my children? Other things? Add to the list above everything the LORD brings to your mind.

How can I unload these heavy burdens that the LORD didn't call me to bear?

Exodus 16:29 ...abide ye every man in his place, let no man go out of his place on the seventh day. This is why observant Jewish people always live within walking distance of their synagogue. It was decided thousands of years ago how far from home a person should be allowed to go and still be in his "place." It is called a "Sabbath Day's journey" which is found in Acts 1:12 **Then returned they unto Jerusalem from the mount called Olivet, which is from Jerusalem a sabbath day's journey.**
This is almost impossible to follow in some of our lives, but it is something to think about and see if the LORD would have us aim for it.

Ex. 34:21 Six days thou shalt work, but on the seventh day thou shalt rest: in earing (planting) **time and in harvest thou shalt rest.**
So, even in busy crunch times, we are still supposed to find time to rest.

Leviticus 19:30 Ye shall keep my Sabbaths, and reverence my sanctuary: I am the LORD.
Leviticus 23:2-3 Speak unto the children of Israel, and say unto them, Concerning the feasts of the LORD, which ye shall <u>proclaim to be holy convocations</u>, even these are my feasts. Six days shall work be done: but the seventh day is the sabbath of rest, <u>an holy convocation</u>; ye shall do no work therein: it is the sabbath of the LORD in all your dwellings.
The LORD considers the Sabbath day one of His special Moadim (Appointed Times)— one of His designated Feast Days. And He says to hold a "holy convocation" on it and to "reverence" His sanctuary.

How does this change my attitude toward the Sabbath and going to worship meetings?

Exodus 31:13 Verily my Sabbaths ye shall keep: for it is a sign between me and you throughout your generations; that ye may know that I am the LORD that doth sanctify you.

How much value does this add to the Sabbath that it is a sign between me and the LORD, that I may get to know Him better, the One who has *sanctified* me (set me apart as a special treasure for Him)?   Use this space to write down what the LORD reveals to you about this. Date your entries and add more as you learn more.

Isaiah 56:1- 8 Thus saith the LORD, Keep ye judgment, and do justice: for my salvation is near to come, and my righteousness to be revealed. Blessed is the man that doeth this, and the son of man that layeth hold on it; that <u>keepeth the sabbath from polluting it</u>, and keepeth his hand from doing any evil. Neither let the son of the stranger, that hath joined himself to the LORD, speak, saying, The LORD hath utterly separated me from His people: neither let the eunuch say, Behold, I am a dry tree. For thus saith the LORD unto the eunuchs that keep my Sabbaths, and choose the things that please me, and take hold of my covenant; Even unto them will I give in mine house and within my walls a place and a name better than of sons and of daughters: I will give them an everlasting name, that shall not be cut off. Also the sons of the stranger, that join themselves to the LORD, to serve him, and to love the name of the LORD, to be his servants, <u>every one that keepeth the Sabbath from polluting it</u>, and taketh hold of My covenant; <u>Even them will I bring to my holy mountain, and make them joyful in My house of prayer</u>: their burnt offerings and their sacrifices shall be accepted upon Mine altar; for Mine house shall be called an house of prayer for all people. The Lord GOD which gathereth the outcasts of Israel saith, Yet will I gather others to him, beside those that are gathered unto him.

How important does this passage make the Sabbath seem?

Is it alright for non-Jewish people to observe the Sabbath?

What rewards are in this passage for keeping the Sabbath?

Isaiah 58:13-14 If thou turn away thy foot from the Sabbath, from doing thy pleasure on my holy day; and call the Sabbath a delight, the holy of the LORD, honourable; and shalt honour him, not doing thine own ways, nor finding thine own pleasure, nor speaking thine own words: Then shalt thou delight thyself in the LORD; and I will cause thee to ride upon the high places of the earth, and feed thee with the heritage of Jacob thy father: for the mouth of the LORD hath spoken it.

Here it suggests not talking so much on the Sabbath. Try it sometime. Spend the day listening to and observing those around you. Speak as little as necessary and even quiet your thoughts. What insights did you gain? Did anyone notice your silence? What special things occurred?

Try it on the Sabbath, spending as much of the day as possible just listening to the LORD. Write down what the LORD reveals to you.

This part of Isaiah 58:13 "**not doing thine own ways, nor finding thine own pleasure,**" could seem like it is taking all the "fun" out of the Sabbath, but that is a very narrow view of God and what He delights in. Isaish 56:4 says, **choose the things that please me.** Wouldn't things that please and delight the LORD be divinely, heavenly joyous? Aren't things He created pleasing to Him? And doesn't our obedience to His commandments bring Him delight? Remember, He commanded people to "be fruitful and multiply" (Gen. 1:22). And read what is commanded in Prov. 5:18-19!

What kinds of things of "finding my own pleasure" would be contrary to Scripture and displeasing to the LORD?

What kinds of pleasurable activities might make the LORD smile and not be against Scripture?

What are the rewards in Isaiah 58:13-14 for keeping the Sabbath?

Jesus healed on the Sabbath:

Matt. 12:12 ... it is lawful to do good on the Sabbath."

Luke 6:9-10 Then Jesus said to them, "I ask you, is it lawful to do good or to do harm on the Sabbath, to save life or to destroy it?"

Luke 13:15 But the Lord answered him and said, "You hypocrites! Does not each of you on the Sabbath untie his ox or his donkey from the manger, and lead it away to give it water? 16 And ought not this woman, a daughter of Abraham whom Satan bound for eighteen long years, be set free from this bondage on the Sabbath day?"

Luke 14:5 5 Then he said to them, "If one of you has a child or an ox that has fallen into a well, will you not immediately pull it out on a Sabbath day?"

John 5:10 -11, 16-17 So the Jews said to the man who had been cured, "It is the Sabbath; it is not lawful for you to carry your mat." 11 But he answered them, "The man who made me well said to me, 'Take up your mat and walk.' " ... 16 Therefore the Jews started persecuting Jesus, because he was doing such things on the Sabbath. 17 But Jesus answered them, "My Father is still working, and I also am working."

What kind of work is Jesus speaking of here?

Is it okay for health care workers and first responders to work on the Sabbath?

Who does the LORD want me to minister His inner and outer healing to this Sabbath?

Ministers don't get to rest on the day that everyone else is resting. Write a prayer for your pastors and spiritual leaders to find time for resting and being refreshed in the LORD.

What does the LORD want me to do to help lighten my pastor's load?

Both Jesus and the Apostle Paul taught in Synagogues on the Sabbath:

Luke 4:14-15 And Jesus returned in the power of the Spirit into Galilee: and there went out a fame of him through all the region round about. And he taught in their synagogues, being glorified of all.

Luke 4:16 And he came to Nazareth, where he had been brought up: and, <u>as his custom was,</u> he went into the synagogue on the Sabbath day, and stood up for to read.

Acts 17:1b-2 ... they came to Thessalonica, where was a synagogue of the Jews: And Paul, <u>as his manner was</u>, went in unto them, and three Sabbath days reasoned with them out of the Scriptures.

What commandment about the Sabbath were they in line with by doing this?
(See page 33, Lev. 23:2-3.)

If Jesus and Paul observed the Sabbath Day this way, ought not I?

Mark 2:27 Then he said to them, "The Sabbath was made for humankind, and not humankind for the Sabbath; 28 so the Son of Man is lord even of the Sabbath."
Luke 6:5 Then he said to them, "The Son of Man is lord of the Sabbath."

Which is more important, the Sabbath or Jesus?

Am I putting my Sabbath observance above my adoration of Jesus?

Which is more important, the Sabbath or people?

According to these passages, why did God create the Sabbath?

Which is more important that I observe the Sabbath to the "T" or that I am rested and refreshed on the Sabbath?

(See Appenices I and II for more about Jesus and Paul and the Sabbath.)

If the Sabbath becomes a burden to us, then we aren't observing it correctly. It might seem like a burden when we first start trying to observe it because we have to change so many things and habits in our lives. Give it a few months until it becomes more routine and then see if it is bringing rest and new energy and a fresh outlook toward the new week.

Use these two pages to keep record of how Sabbath goes the first few months. (Coordinate this with your list on pages 24-25.) Write down how you felt during and afterward, so you can see the progression of the benefits and the rewards from the LORD.

Acts 20:7- 11 And upon the first *day* of the week, when the disciples came together to break bread, Paul preached unto them, ready to depart on the morrow; and continued his speech until midnight. And <u>there were many lights in the upper chamber, where they were gathered together.</u>

Now that we know that the Hebrew day begins at sundown, we know that this event occurred on Saturday evening and night. In Israel, gathering to eat together when the Sabbath is over (at dusk) is the customary thing to do! Ben Yehudah street in Jerusalem (an outdoor mall, no cars street) that was empty and quiet all day is suddenly full of people shopping and eating! Notice it says **"there were many lights ... where they were gathered."** They needed light because it was at sundown when the Sabbath ends and the first day of the week begins! There is a sense of celebration in the air at this time. It's like some free time before the work week begins. In America, if you keep Sabbath on the seventh day, you have a whole day of free time before the work week begins.

Who would the LORD like me to celebrate with on the evening after Sabbath? Date your entry. Then record later how the celebrations went and how you felt.

Observing the Sabbath is between you and the LORD only. It is not open for others to judge us or for us to judge others:
Col 2:16 Let no man therefore judge you in meat, or in drink, or in respect of an holyday, or of the new moon, or of the Sabbath days:

Romans 14:4 Who art thou that judgest another man's servant?

Some people esteem every day as holy as the Sabbath.
Romans 14:4-6 Who art thou that judgest another man's servant? to his own master he standeth or falleth. Yea, he shall be holden up: for God is able to make him stand. 5 One man esteemeth one day above another: another esteemeth every day alike. Let every man be fully persuaded in his own mind. 6 He that regardeth the day, regardeth it unto the Lord; and he that regardeth not the day, to the Lord he doth not regard it.

It is not for us to judge others about their Sabbath practices. We just need to listen to the LORD and do what He says for *us* to do. Make sure we are fulfilling His desire and calling for us and not just doing things our own way. Everything we do on the Sabbath or on any other day is for Him!

It's time for some real soul searching.
What is my tendency concerning the Sabbath?

Am I quick to resist observing the Sabbath and not want to be constrained by it? Is this attitude from the LORD? Or does it stem from a bit of a rebellious streak still inside me?

Am I one to quickly plunge into Sabbath observance (and adherence to other commandments) and get really strict and rigid about it until it becomes a burden to me and those around me?

Are other people possibly hesitant to talk to me about things like the Sabbath because of my strong opinions?

Do I take time to listen to their heart without showing any judging attitude toward them?

When have I possibly shown a critical attitude toward someone? Write an apology and a prayer asking God for forgiveness.

Am I looking down my nose at anyone who doesn't see the Sabbath the way I do, even though I don't say anything? Who and why? Write an apology and a prayer asking God for forgiveness.

Honor thy father and thy mother

What does this commandment mean to me?

How have I been keeping this commandment?

How have I been breaking this commandment?

What does it feel like to be honored by my children?

What kinds of things make me feel honored?

What have I done lately that felt honoring to my father?

What can I do today that will feel honoring to him?

What have I done lately that felt honoring to my mother?

What can I do today that will feel honoring to her?

Does this commandment include grandparents? How can I honor them?

Does this commandment include step parents? How can I show them honor?

Does this commandment include honoring the elderly? How can I show honor to the elderly in my life.

Does this commandment include the forefathers of our faith? List important ones to you. How have I been honoring or dishonoring them?

How am I honoring the founders of our country?

How have I been honoring or dishonoring today's leaders of our country? List them and write a prayer for them.

The reading primer of the 1800s says this commandment includes honoring those in authority.

Who are those in authority in my life?

Am I showing honor to those who have authority over me?

How do I treat policemen when I see them or when they give me a ticket?

Do I gossip about my pastor and his family?

How about other church leaders?

How have I spoken respectfully about my pastor?

How do I talk about my children's teachers and coaches, etc?

List all the people in authority over you that God lays on your heart and write down how you speak about them and treat them, and how you can show them honor. Ask the LORD to give you Bible verses to pray over them.

That thy days may be long

Think about the elderly people you know. (List them) How do they speak about their parents? (Write it down next to their names.)

How can I help make sure I live a long life?

That it may go well with thee... (Ephesians 6:3)

How have things been going in my life lately?

If things have not been going well, could it have something to do with how I am honoring my parents and others?

In the land that the LORD thy God giveth thee

Has the LORD given me any land? A home? Could this have anything to do with how much honor I am giving my parents and others?

What if my parent was abusive? What if one is not a good person? Do I still need to honor them? Well, there is no clause in this commandment that says, honor them, unless they are bad people. So how can I honor a bad parent?

Would forgiving them be honoring to them? Write a prayer of forgiveness. Pray it several times a day until you no longer feel the pain or anger from what they did to you.

Example: LORD Jesus, I forgive _____ for doing this to me: _____. I release them from owing me anything. I turn them and my anger over to you. I pray You will bless them.

Would telling them I forgive them, honor them? Write what you could say as forgiveness.

Would not letting their bad traits influence you be honoring? How can I make sure of this? Write a prayer asking the LORD to help you in this.

Would it honor them for their child (me) to turn out to be a good person in spite of how they treated me? Write a prayer.

Would it honor them if I could lead them to their Savior? Write a prayer for them. Never give up in believing for their salvation.

Ask the LORD to give you Bible verses to pray over them:

Why does the LORD require that we honor our parents? Would I even exist without them? He chose to use them to create me. How should I feel about that?

FIRST COMMANDMENT re-check

MIND: When I let my mind wander, where does it go?

SOUL: The Hebrew word "nefish" comes from the root word meaning "take a breath." Do I love the LORD with my every breath? Our voice requires our breath. What did I use my voice for today? Yelling? Singing praises? Criticizing? Encouraging others?

Am I **always prepared** with my words to "**give a reason for the hope**" that is in me? (I Peter 3:15 NIV) List some brief ways you can tell about your personal hope in Jesus.

HEART: Who has my heart *today* or *yesterday*?

STRENGTH: In Hebrew this word is "maod" (pronounced may-ode). "Tov maod" means "very good." ["Tov" meaning "good" rhymes with "stove."] "Maod" can mean "very, <u>exceedingly</u>, <u>greatly</u>, much, might, force, <u>abundance</u>, muchness ... <u>diligently</u>, mightily..." So the question for me today is: Am I loving the LORD diligently out of my abundance? Am I loving Him exceedingly and greatly?

The Hebrew root word of "maod" is "ode" which means "ember."

Is my love for the LORD always as hot as glowing embers, ready to burst into flames with any added fuel?

Do I keep adding the fuel I need to keep those coals burning hot or do I add things that quench the fire?

What things tend to cool my coals?

What is the fuel I personally need to keep burning hot for the LORD?

Is part of it spending time with Him, studying His Word? Have I done that lately? What's the most significant thing I've learned from His Word lately?

How about meeting with other people who love Him? Is there a Bible study I should be attending? Or leading?

THE SECOND GREAT COMMANDMENT: LOVE THY NEIGHBOR AS THYSELF

And the second is like, namely this,

Thou shalt love thy neighbour

as thyself.

There is none other commandment

greater than these.

Mark 12:31

How have I been loving people in my life?

Who have I been having trouble loving?

Who is my neighbor? Read Jesus' parable about the Good Samaritan (Luke 10:25-37). Is my neighbor maybe anyone who needs my help? Who is that in my life?

Is someone in a different social group than mine, even if despised by me or others, still my neighbor? Who is that in my life?

Is someone who offends me also one of my neighbors?   Who is that for me?

Matt. 18:21 Lord, how oft shall my brother sin against me, and I forgive him?

Is forgiving someone, loving them? List people you need to forgive. Write a prayer of forgiveness for each one.

Example: Lord Jesus, I forgive _____ for doing this to me: _____

_____. I release them

from owing me anything. I turn them and my anger and inner pain over to you. I pray You will bless them.

Matt. 5:44 Love your enemies, bless them that curse you, do good to them that hate you, and pray for them which despitefully use you, and persecute you.

List those who feel like enemies to you. Write a prayer of blessing over each one, including that they come to know the LORD and grow closer to Him.

Luke 6:31 (NIV) Do to others as you would have them do to you...

Is following the Golden Rule showing love?

What would I like my neighbor to do for me?

What would I like my "enemy" to do for me? Write the answers beside the people on the above two lists on these two pages. Should I maybe try to do those things for them? (Make sure it is something they would actually like. People like different things.)

Love thy neighbor **as thyself**
Do I love myself?

Why do I not like myself? List all the ways. Then write down the truth of what the Father says about each one.
Example:
What I don't like: I did this really bad thing_____
God's Truth: The Father forgives me for this. Jesus shed His blood for this. Were the nails in His hands not big enough and the stripes on His back not deep enough for this particular sin? Am I saying the Jesus needed to suffer more in order for God to forgive me for this?

I John 4:19 (NIV) We love because He first loved us....
Do I know the Father loves me? Do I know it deep inside myself? Am I secure in His love?

Eph. 3:18-19 May be able to comprehend ... the breadth, and length, and depth, and height; and to know the love of Christ.
Write a prayer asking the LORD to show you in a real, amazing way how much He loves you.

Write down verses about the Father's love that He gives you. Ponder them. Say them out loud to yourself over and over until you feel it for sure deep inside you and it cannot be shaken from you.

Thou shalt not kill

What did Jesus say this commandment means?

Matt. 5:21-22 **Ye have heard that it was said by them of old time, Thou shalt not kill; and whosoever shall kill shall be in danger of the judgment: But I say unto you, That whosoever is angry with his brother without a cause shall be in danger of the judgment: and whosoever shall say to his brother, Raca, shall be in danger of the council: but whosoever shall say, Thou fool, shall be in danger of hell fire.**

Who do I have anger in my heart toward?

Matt. 5:23-24 **Therefore if thou bring thy gift to the altar, and there rememberest that thy brother hath ought against thee; Leave there thy gift before the altar, and go thy way; first be reconciled to thy brother, and then come and offer thy gift.**

According to this, our anger affects our worship toward God. How can I reconcile to the person I am angry with?

How about someone who is angry with me?

Matt. 5:25-26 **Agree with thine adversary quickly, whiles thou art in the way with him; lest at any time the adversary deliver thee to the judge, and the judge deliver thee to the officer, and thou be cast into prison. Verily I say unto thee, Thou shalt by no means come out thence, till thou hast paid the uttermost farthing.**

Is my anger keeping my soul and emotions in prison?

How is my anger affecting my life, my emotions, my attitude towards life?

How is my anger affecting my family?

Thou shalt not commit adultery

What did Jesus say this commandment means?

Matt. 5:27-30 **Ye have heard that it was said by them of old time, Thou shalt not commit adultery: But I say unto you, That whosoever looketh on a woman to lust after her hath committed adultery with her already in his heart. And if thy right eye offend thee, pluck it out, and cast it from thee: for it is profitable for thee that one of thy members should perish, and not that thy whole body should be cast into hell. And if thy right hand offend thee, cut it off, and cast it from thee: for it is profitable for thee that one of thy members should perish, and not that thy whole body should be cast into hell.**

When have I gazed too long at an attractive person until it caused me to lust?

Am I harboring lust in my heart?

What things cause me to lust? Movies? Internet videos and websites? Flirting? List them all. How can I avoid ("cut off") each of them?

Billy Graham made sure he never spent any time alone with another woman. When have I tempted myself (or tempted the other person) by paying too much attention to them? Spending too much time with them? Flirting or joking around too much with them? Spending time alone with them? How can I stop doing these things?

Thou shalt not steal

What all kinds of things can be stolen?

What have I ever stolen?

When and how did I repent of this so that God can forgive me?

How did I make restitution for my stealing?

Lev. 6:2-5 NRSV **When any of you sin and commit a trespass against the LORD by deceiving a neighbor in a matter of a deposit or a pledge, or by robbery, or if you have defrauded a neighbor, or have found something lost and lied about it—if you swear falsely regarding any of the various things that one may do and sin thereby—when you have sinned and realize your guilt, and would restore what you took by robbery or by fraud or the deposit that was committed to you, or the lost thing that you found, or anything else about which you have sworn falsely, you shall repay the principal amount and shall add one-fifth to it. You shall pay it to its owner when you realize your guilt.**

According to this Bible passage, what are all the ways a person can steal?

Through **deceit**: When might I have ever deceived anyone?

Through **fraud** (this is deception for the purpose of financial gain): Are my business transactions always totally honest and up front?

Through **lost** and **found**: "Finders keepers, losers weepers" is NOT in the Bible! Is there anything I'm keeping that belongs to someone else that I haven't returned to them?

Lev. 6:5b ... **you shall repay the principal amount and shall add one-fifth to it.**

How much restitution does God require for things stolen?

What restitution do I need to rectify by giving back more than I took?

What might I have stolen from God?

Malachi 3:8-12 **Will a man rob God? Yet ye have robbed Me. But ye say, Wherein have we robbed Thee? In tithes and offerings. Ye _are_ cursed with a curse: for ye have robbed Me, _even_ this whole nation. Bring ye all the tithes into the storehouse, that there may be meat in Mine house, and prove me now herewith, saith the LORD of hosts, if I will not open you the windows of heaven, and pour you out a blessing, that _there shall_ not _be room_ enough _to receive it._**

The Hebrew words of the last phrase are "brakhah od-bli-di" which can mean "an endless blessing."

How have things been going lately in my life? Does it feel more like it's "cursed" rather than blessed? If so, have I been giving my whole tithe lately?

What "offerings" in addition to my tithes have I given lately?

2 Corinthians 9:6-7 **But this *I say*, He which soweth sparingly shall reap also sparingly; and he which soweth bountifully shall reap also bountifully. Every man according as he purposeth in his heart, so let him give; not grudgingly, or of necessity: for God loveth a cheerful giver.**

What has been my attitude toward tithes and offerings? Could this have anything to do with why I am not being blessed?

Here's a list of my income and my tithing to prove I am giving the correct amount:

Luke 6:38 **Give, and it shall be given unto you; good measure, pressed down, and shaken together, and running over, shall men give into your bosom. For with the same measure that ye mete withal it shall be measured to you again.**

What kind of giver have I been?

Matt. 6:19-21 **Lay not up for yourselves treasures upon earth, where moth and rust doth corrupt, and where thieves break through and steal: But lay up for yourselves treasures in heaven, where neither moth nor rust doth corrupt, and where thieves do not break through nor steal: For where your treasure is, there will your heart be also.**

Have I been robbing from myself from my treasure in heaven?

Where is my heart focused most of the time? Is it tied up in possessions?

What "treasures" do I have here on earth that I could give to others, so my heart will be less on this earth and more focused on heavenly and spiritual things? Make a list of each item and who it could be given to.

Thou shalt not bear false witness against thy neighbor

When have I ever hurt anyone by telling a lie?

When have I hurt someone by just shading the truth a little bit?

When have I exaggerated or slightly twisted the truth to make myself look better than someone else? Or just spoken negatively about them?

About my parents? (This would be breaking two commandments.)

About my spouse?

About my kids?

About my siblings?

About my peers or other Christians?

When have I listened to gossip?

When have I continued the gossip?

When have I started gossip?

When have I stopped someone from telling me gossip?

When have I stopped a gossip with the truth?

Why is it that we humans are so quick to judge others and put them down? Including doctors and nurses who have taken care of our loved ones or other professionals, such as lawyers, teachers, or the police. Why do we think we have a right to condemn them? They are only human. They make mistakes. They deserve our kindness and our prayers just like everyone else. When have I spoken negatively about professional people?

What professional people in my life should I be speaking kindly of and praying for?

Ephesians 4:12-15 **For the perfecting of the saints, for the work of the ministry, for the edifying of the body of Christ: Till we all come in the unity of the faith, and of the knowledge of the Son of God, unto a perfect man, unto the measure of the stature of the fullness of Christ: That we** *henceforth* **be no more children, tossed to and fro, and carried about with every wind of doctrine, by the sleight of men, and cunning craftiness, whereby they lie in wait to deceive; But SPEAKING THE TRUTH IN LOVE, may grow up into him in all things, which is the head,** *even* **Christ:**

What "truth" is being referred to here? Is it the Truth of God's Word?

Who can I speak a Scriptural Truth in love to today to help them grow in Christ?

Truth and love and honor are the opposite of lies and gossip. Romans 12:10 NRSV **Love one another with mutual affection; outdo one another in showing honor.**

Whom have I been honoring?

Who can I honor this week and how? Make a list.

Thou shalt not covet
What do I want that I don't have?

Thou shalt not covet thy neighbor's house
When have I complained and felt jealous because other people have better homes than I do?

Thou shalt not covet thy neighbor's wife
When have I wished in my heart that my spouse was more like so and so?

When have I wished my marriage was more like the marriage of so and so?

Am I constantly saying and thinking that my marriage could be better? (This might be making my spouse feel unloved or disrespected.)

Nor his manservant, nor his maidservant
When have I thought that other people have a better dishwasher or stove or washer and dryer or better lawnmower or leaf blower or better tools or better cell phones or laptops or ipads ....? How about better income?!

Nor his ox, nor his donkey

What could this represent today?

When have I been jealous of the cars other people have?

Nor any thing that is thy neighbor's
I'm listing all the things I've been jealous of or wished I had something better than I have. Then as I repent and get my heart unhooked from coveting each one, I will date it and cross it off the list.

Luke 3:14b ... **and be content with your wages.**
Philippians 4:11 **Not that I speak in respect of want: for I have learned, in whatsoever state I am, *therewith* to be content.**
I Timothy 6:8 **And having food and raiment let us be therewith content.**
Hebrews 13:5 *Let your* **conversation** *be* **without covetousness;** *and be* **content with such things as ye have: for he hath said, I will never leave thee, nor forsake thee.**
Psalm 23:1 **The LORD** *is* **my shepherd I shall not want.**
Philippians 4:19 **But my God shall supply all your need according to his riches in glory by Christ Jesus.**
Psalm 69:30-31 **I will praise the name of God with a song, and will magnify Him with thanksgiving.** *This* **also shall please the LORD better than an ox** *or* **bullock that hath horns and hoofs.** (And ox or bull were the biggest sacrifices a person could give to the LORD. They were used for burnt offerings which were not for atoning for sin, but were for the sole purpose of worshiping Him.)

Coveting and complaining shows that we don't trust the LORD to provide for us and we aren't happy with what He has given us. Giving thanks is the opposite of complaining or coveting. Giving thanks is the cure for covetousness. What can I thank God for today?

On the list above of things you've coveted, write what you are thankful for that will cure your coveting of that item.

Use the next two pages to begin listing thankfulness to the LORD.

I'M THANKFUL FOR:

I'M THANKFUL FOR:

FIRST COMMANDMENT re-check in more depth

MIND: The Greek word used for this in the New Testament "dianoia" can also mean "understanding" or "way of thinking."

Am I doing everything I can to learn to understand the LORD? To understand the Scripture He gave us? To understand His Ways? What can I do to keep increasing my understanding of Him? List them.

Begin to list the revelations and insights He gives you from your study of His Word. Date each one as you add them.

Does my way of thinking line up with His Word? Where have I been getting my philosophy and world view? From God and His Word? Or from the internet? Or from college professors? Where? Make a list. Do research to find out where the beliefs came from. Write dates. Add to this list as you learn more about the LORD.

SOUL: They say our soul is where our emotions are. What have my emotions been like lately?

Are my emotions coming from my love for the LORD?

Do I have anxiety or fears or worry? Are those emotions telling me lies about the LORD? On this page and the next, list all the things , no matter how insignificant, that bring you anxiety or worry or fear.

Beside each one, write what you are believing about it that makes you afraid.

Then find a Bible verse that tells the truth about it. Read the verse over and over aloud every time that anxiety comes back. Keep doing this until you believe deep inside the truth of God's Word about that. Eventually the anxiety or fear won't come anymore.

Be thoroughly honest. List every last fear or worry, no matter how long the list. Use the extra blank pages at the end of this book and/or extra paper, if needed. Being set free from worry and anxiety and fear is so worth it!

ALL MY FEARS AND ANXIETY:

ALL MY FEARS AND ANXIETY (every last one):

STRENGTH: The Greek word "yschis" can mean "strength, power, might, ability."

Ability: How have I been using my abilities and talents and gifts for the LORD's glory? List them and write how you've been using them.

Power: Am I using my position of power or authority for the LORD? Am I using it the way He has called me to use it?

As a parent?

As a teacher?

Other:

Who and what do I have power or authority over? List them. Write how in each case I can bring glory to the LORD.

Luke 10:19 **Behold, I give unto you power to tread on serpents and scorpions, and over all the power of the enemy: and nothing shall by any means hurt you.**
Revelations 12:9-10 **And I heard a loud voice saying in heaven, Now is come salvation, and strength, and the kingdom of our God, and the power of his Christ: for the accuser of our brethren is cast down, which accused them before our God day and night. And THEY OVERCAME HIM BY THE BLOOD OF THE LAMB, AND BY THE WORD OF THEIR TESTIMONY; and they loved not their lives unto the death.**

Am I using the power and authority Jesus gave me over the devil in the way He designed? Am I using it at all?

How has the enemy been accusing me in my thoughts? Make a list. I can combat each negative thought with the Truth of God's Word. Write a Scripture that tells the truth about each of the enemy's lies.

Matthew 21:21 **Jesus answered and said unto them, Verily I say unto you, If ye have faith, and doubt not, ye shall not only do this *which is done* to the fig tree, but also if ye shall say unto this mountain, Be thou removed, and be thou cast into the sea; it shall be done.**

Mark 11:23 **For verily I say unto you, That whosoever shall say unto this mountain, Be thou removed, and be thou cast into the sea; and shall not doubt in his heart, but shall believe that those things which he saith shall come to pass; he shall have whatsoever he saith.**

Mark 17:6 **And the Lord said, If ye had faith as a grain of mustard seed, ye might say unto this sycamine tree, Be thou plucked up by the root, and be thou planted in the sea; and it should obey you.**

John 15:7-8a **If ye abide in Me, and My Words abide in you, ye shall ask what ye will, and it shall be done unto you. Herein is My Father glorified**, ...

What things in my life could be there because the devil is trying to defeat me? Sickness, misfortune, troubles, etc. List them and take authority over them in Jesus' Name by the power of His blood and tell them to "be removed and cast into the sea." Write the date. Keep doing this over and over. Date when they are gone. Give God all the glory. This is one way to Love Him with all our strength and glorify Him.

HEART: Is there anything I'm holding above God in my heart *today*?

Colossians 3:23-24 NIV **Whatever you do, WORK AT IT WITH ALL YOUR HEART, as working for the Lord, not for human masters, since you know that you will receive an inheritance from the Lord as a reward. It is the Lord Christ you are serving.**

What work am I doing for JESUS?

What things am I doing just out of duty or just because I'm supposed to and my heart isn't in it?

What things am I doing that the LORD hasn't called me to do which is why my heart isn't in it? How can I make plans and arrangements so I can quit doing these things?

What things do I need to get a better heart attitude about? Write a prayer beside each one.

What things has the LORD called me to do that I am not doing yet? (Spend time before the LORD, listening to Him for what He has called you to do. Write it all down.) How can I put my faith in Him and arrange my life so that I can obey Him with my whole heart? (If it seems impossible write down a prayer for what needs to change so it can come to pass. Date this prayer. Then write down what happens in answer to that prayer and date the answer.)

Final, bonus question:
Jesus gave us a test to see if we love Him:

John 14:15 If ye love Me, keep My commandments.

John 14:12 He that hath My commandments, and keepeth them, he it is that loveth Me: and he that loveth Me shall be loved of My Father, and I will love him, and will manifest Myself to him.

John 14:23 If a man love Me, he will keep My Words: and My Father will love him, and we will come unto him, and make Our abode with him.

Now that you have been making sure you are obeying the Ten Commandments, have you been feeling closer to the LORD and sensing His Love more and more? (If you haven't yet, keep your antenna up to be more aware of this.)

Do you sense His presence more in your life?

As the LORD brings other commandments from Scripture to your mind, write them down and check your life to see if you have been obeying them. If not, ask Him for forgiveness, then record how and when you start obeying them. Then record how Jesus begins to come to you and to reveal Himself more to you, and what more blessings begin to flow.

APPENDIX I

IS THE GOD I WORSHIP THE ONE TRUE GOD OF THE BIBLE?

Is there only one true God? Isaiah 43:11; Isaiah 45:5; Isaiah 46:9

Does God have a Son? Proverbs 30:4
Who is His Son? Matthew 3:17; Luke 3:22; Matthew 17:5

Are God and Jesus one God? John 10:30; John 14:7,9

Is there anything more powerful than God? Jeremiah 32:17,27; Ephesians 1:19-22;
Philippians 2:9-11;

Who created the whole world, including me? Genesis chapters 1-3; Nehemiah 9:6;
John 1:3; Colossians 1:15-16; Psalm 139:13-15

Does God know everything? Isaiah 46:9-10; I John 3:20

Does God know my thoughts? Psalm 139:1-4; Matthew 12:25; Luke 5:22; Luke 11:17;
Hebrews 4:13

Does God think like me? Isaiah 55:8-9

Where is God? Jeremiah 23:24; Psalm 139:7-12

When does God and His Law become old and outdated? Numbers 23:19; Psalm 33:11;
Malachi 3:6; Hebrews 13:8

Is God a loving God? I John 4:8

Does He care about me? I Peter 5:7

What's the biggest thing God did to show His love? Write the whole verse John 3:16

What makes God angry? Exodus 15:7; Numbers 11:1-2; Romans 1:18; Romans 2:5; Ephesians 5:3-6

Does God judge evil people? 1 Corinthians 6:9-10 Galatians 5:19-21; Revelation 22:12-16

Does God forgive? John 3:17-18; Ephesians 2:4-6, 8-9,

What does God require before He will forgive? Acts 16:31; Romans 10:9-10; I John 1:9

If I want to know God and put Him first in my life, what will He do for me? Jeremiah 29:12-13; Jeremiah 33:3; Proverbs 3:6; Proverbs 16:3; Colossians 3:1-4

Does God have a plan for my life? Psalm 139:16; Jeremiah 29:11; Ephesians 2:10

APPENDIX II

JESUS AND THE SABBATH:

Matthew 12:11-13, 15b He said to them, "Suppose one of you has only one sheep and it falls into a pit on the Sabbath; will you not lay hold of it and lift it out? 12 How much more valuable is a human being than a sheep! So it is lawful to do good on the Sabbath." 13 Then he said to the man, "Stretch out your hand." He stretched it out, and it was restored, as sound as the other. ... Many crowds followed him, and he cured all of them,

Mark 1:21 ... and straightway on the sabbath day he entered into the synagogue, and taught.

Mark 6:2a And when the sabbath day was come, he began to teach in the synagogue.

Luke 4:14-15 And Jesus returned in the power of the Spirit into Galilee: and there went out a fame of him through all the region round about. And he taught in their synagogues, being glorified of all.

Luke 4:16 And he came to Nazareth, where he had been brought up: and, as his custom was, he went into the synagogue on the Sabbath day, and stood up for to read.

Luke 4:31 And came down to Capernaum, a city of Galilee, and taught them on the Sabbath days.

Luke 6:6 On another Sabbath he entered the synagogue and taught....

Luke 13:10 And he was teaching in one of the synagogues on the sabbath.

Mark 2:27 Then he said to them, "The Sabbath was made for humankind, and not humankind for the Sabbath; 28 so the Son of Man is lord even of the Sabbath."
Luke 6:5 Then he said to them, "The Son of Man is lord of the Sabbath."

Mark 3:3-5 And he said to the man who had the withered hand, "Come forward." 4 Then he said to them, "Is it lawful to do good or to do harm on the Sabbath, to save life or to kill?" But they were silent. 5 He looked around at them with anger; he was grieved at their hardness of heart and said to the man, "Stretch out your hand." He stretched it out, and his hand was restored.

Luke 6:9-10 Then Jesus said to them, "I ask you, is it lawful to do good or to do harm on the Sabbath, to save life or to destroy it?" 10 After looking around at all of them, he said to him, "Stretch out your hand." He did so, and his hand was restored.

Luke 13:10-17 Now he was teaching in one of the synagogues on the Sabbath. 11 And just then there appeared a woman with a spirit that had crippled her for eighteen years. She was bent over and was quite unable to stand up straight. 12 When Jesus saw her, he called her over and said, "Woman, you are set free from your ailment." 13 When he laid his hands on her, immediately she stood up straight and began praising God. 14 But the leader of the synagogue, indignant because Jesus had cured on the Sabbath, kept saying to the crowd, "There are six days on which work ought to be done; come on those days and be cured, and not on the Sabbath day." 15 But the Lord answered him and said, "You hypocrites! Does not each of you on the Sabbath untie his ox or his donkey from the manger, and lead it away to give it water? 16 And ought not this woman, a daughter of Abraham whom Satan bound for eighteen long years, be set free from this bondage on the Sabbath day?" 17 When he said this, all his opponents were put to shame; and the entire crowd was rejoicing at all the wonderful things that he was doing.

Luke 14:1-6 On one occasion when Jesus was going to the house of a leader of the Pharisees to eat a meal on the Sabbath, they were watching him closely. 2 Just then, in front of him, there was a man who had dropsy. 3 And Jesus asked the lawyers and Pharisees, "Is it lawful to cure people on the Sabbath, or not?" 4 But they were silent. So Jesus took him and healed him, and sent him away. 5 Then he said to them, "If one of you has a child or an ox that has fallen into a well, will you not immediately pull it out on a Sabbath day?" 6 And they could not reply to this.

John 5:8-9, 16   Jesus said to him, "Stand up, take your mat and walk." 9 At once the man was made well, and he took up his mat and began to walk. Now that day was a Sabbath. 10 So the Jews said to the man who had been cured, "It is the Sabbath; it is not lawful for you to carry your mat." 11 But he answered them, "The man who made me well said to me, "Take up your mat and walk.' " ... 16 Therefore the Jews started persecuting Jesus, because he was doing such things on the Sabbath. 17 But Jesus answered them, "My Father is still working, and I also am working."

John 7:21-24 Jesus answered them, "I performed one work, and all of you are astonished. 22 Moses gave you circumcision (it is, of course, not from Moses, but from the patriarchs), and you circumcise a man on the Sabbath. 23 If a man receives circumcision on the Sabbath in order that the law of Moses may not be broken, are you angry with me because I healed a man's whole body on the Sabbath? 24 Do not judge by appearances, but judge with right judgment."

John 9:6-7, **When he had said this, he spat on the ground and made mud with the saliva and spread the mud on the man's eyes, 7 saying to him, "Go, wash in the pool of Siloam" (which means Sent). Then he went and washed and came back able to see. ... 14 Now it was a Sabbath day when Jesus made the mud and opened his eyes. ... 16 Some of the Pharisees said, "This man is not from God, for he does not observe the Sabbath." But others said, "How can a man who is a sinner perform such signs?" And they were divided.**

Did Jesus do away with the Law?
Matthew 5:17-19 **Think not that I am come to destroy the <u>law, or the prophets</u>: I am not come to destroy, but to fulfill. For verily I say unto you, Till heaven and earth pass, one jot or one tittle shall in no wise pass from the law, till all be fulfilled. Whosoever therefore shall break one of these least commandments, and shall teach men so, he shall be called the least in the Kingdom of Heaven: but whosoever shall do and teach them, the same shall be called great in the Kingdom of Heaven.**

Matthew 5:20 **For I say unto you, That except your righteousness shall exceed the righteousness of the scribes and Pharisees, ye shall in no case enter into the kingdom of heaven.**
The Pharisees were a group started by Ezra with the goal to teach people to follow the Torah (the first 5 books of the Bible). They were devoted to following God. Over the years they put "fences" around each commandment to help make sure people didn't break them. By Jesus' time, for some of them, the focus was on those fences more than on God, so much so that they wanted to put Jesus to death for not observing the Sabbath according to those "fences." Is Jesus telling us not to obey the commandments? Or is He telling us to obey them, while keeping our focus on God and His mercy and His intent behind the Torah? The Torah actually points to Jesus and His sacrifice which washes away our sins, fulfilling all of the *animal* sacrificial requirements.

APPENDIX III

PAUL AND THE APOSTLES ON THE SABBATH

The Apostles and new believers went to the Synagogues on the Sabbath it appears:

Act. 13:27 For they that dwell at Jerusalem, and their rulers, because they knew him not, nor yet the voices of the prophets which are read every sabbath day,

Acts 15:21 For Moses of old time hath in every city them that preach him, being read in the synagogues every sabbath day.

Apostle Paul went to Synagogues every Sabbath and taught until he was kicked out, but he continued to teach on the Sabbaths:

Acts 13:42, 44 And when the Jews were gone out of the synagogue, the Gentiles besought that these words might be preached to them the next Sabbath. ... And the next Sabbath day came almost the whole city together to hear the word of God.

Acts 16:13 And on the Sabbath we went out of the city by a river side, where prayer was wont to be made; and we sat down, and spake unto the women which resorted thither.

Acts 17:1b-2   ... they came to Thessalonica, where was a synagogue of the Jews: And Paul, as his manner was, went in unto them, and three Sabbath days reasoned with them out of the Scriptures.

Acts 18:4 And he reasoned in the synagogue every Sabbath, and persuaded the Jews and the Greeks.

Acts 20:7- 11 And upon the first *day* of the week, when the disciples came together to break bread, Paul preached unto them, ready to depart on the morrow; and continued his speech until midnight. And <u>there were many lights in the upper chamber, where they were gathered together.</u> And there sat in a window a certain young man named Eutychus, being fallen into a deep sleep: and as Paul was long preaching, he sunk down with sleep, and fell down from the third loft, and was taken up dead. And Paul went down, and fell on him, and embracing *him* said, Trouble not yourselves; for his life is in him. When he therefore was come up again, and had broken bread, and eaten, and talked a long while, even till break of day, so he departed.

Now that we know that the Hebrew day begins at sundown, we know that this event occurred on Saturday evening and all night. In Israel, gathering to eat together at dusk after the Sabbath is over is the customary thing to do! Ben Yehudah street in Jerusalem (an outdoor mall) in the evening as soon as the Sabbath is over is suddenly full of people shopping and eating! Notice the words we underlined in the Scripture in Acts say "there were many lights ... where they were gathered." They would have needed light from the beginning of the meeting because it was at sundown when the Sabbath ends and the first day of the week begins!

Observing the Sabbath is between you and the LORD only. It is not open for others to judge us or us to judge others:

Col 2:16 Let no man therefore judge you in meat, or in drink, or in respect of an holyday, or of the new moon, or of the Sabbath days:

Romans 14:4 Who art thou that judgest another man's servant?

Some people esteem every day as holy as the Sabbath.

Romans 14:4-6 Who art thou that judgest another man's servant? to his own master he standeth or falleth. Yea, he shall be holden up: for God is able to make him stand. 5 One man esteemeth one day above another: another esteemeth every day alike. Let every man be fully persuaded in his own mind. 6 He that regardeth the day, regardeth it unto the Lord; and he that regardeth not the day, to the Lord he doth not regard it.

It is not for us to judge others about their Sabbath practices. We just need to listen to the LORD and do what He says for us to do.

Thank you for studying the Ten Commandments using this *Journal*. If it has blessed you in any way, we would appreciate your taking a moment to write a review on Amazon, and then copying and pasting it on other sites like Barnes and Noble, Christian Book, Olive Press Publisher, and on social media. If we get 50 reviews on Amazon, then Amazon will include the *Ten Commandments Journal* in their promotions, such as, "Customers who bought this item also bought...."

We thank you for helping this book get the exposure it needs!

Ten Commandments Journal

is available at:

olivepresspublisher.com

amazon.com

barnesandnoble.com

christianbook.com

and other online stores

Store managers:

Order wholesale through:

Ingram Book Company or

Spring Arbor

or by emailing:

olivepressbooks@gmail.com

Other Bible studies by this author:

Online:

olivepresspublisher.com/wp/insights/

In Books:

Endtimes Scripture Handbook for Powerful, Strategic Praying
God's Plan for Ishmael
The Glory of Torah: All the Commandments Organized

www.ingramcontent.com/pod-product-compliance
Lightning Source LLC
Chambersburg PA
CBHW081419090426
42738CB00017B/3423